This Book Belongs To

Made in the USA
Monee, IL
04 August 2020

37613658R00063